Contents

I am a teacher.

Welcome to school!

5

My job is to help you learn.

I teach many **subjects**.

Math is fun.

Who wants to solve
this **problem**?

Gym class helps you
stay healthy.

Stretch those **muscles** first!

11

We learn about the world in **geography** class.

Do you know where you live?

Learning can make you hungry.

Time for lunch!

Let's go to the **cafeteria**.

We practice reading and writing.

That's a good sentence!

Computers can help
you learn.

I will show you how to
use one.

18

19

When you go home,
I grade your papers.

Then I plan your lessons
for tomorrow!

21

New Words

cafeteria (kaff-uh-TEER-ree-ah) A place to buy and eat food.

geography (jee-AH-grah-fee) The natural parts of an area.

muscles (MUSS-sels) Tissue in your body that makes you move.

problem (PRAH-blum) A math question to solve.

subjects (SUB-jekts) Topics taught in school, such as math, history, and art.

Index

About the Author

Erika de Nijs played college hockey before becoming a teacher and a writer. Her parents are from the Netherlands, but she grew up in Upstate New York.

About BOOKWORMS

Bookworms help independent readers gain reading confidence through high-frequency words, simple sentences, and strong picture/text support. Each book explores a concept that helps children relate what they read to the world in which they live.